This Book Belongs To

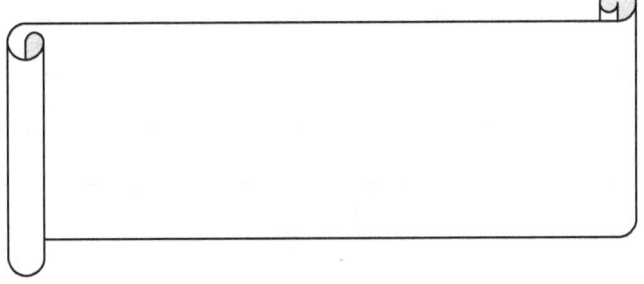

Notes

Notes

Notes

Notes

Notes

Notes

Notes

Notes

Notes

Notes

Notes

Notes

Notes

Notes

Notes

Notes

Notes

Notes

Notes

Notes

Notes

Notes

Notes

Notes

Notes

Notes

Notes

Notes

Notes

Notes

Notes

Notes

Notes

Notes

Notes

Notes

Notes

Notes

Notes

Notes

Notes

Notes

Notes

Notes

Notes

Notes

Notes

Notes

Notes

Notes

Notes

Notes

Notes

Notes

Notes

Notes

Notes

Notes

Notes

Notes

Notes

Notes

Notes

Notes

Notes

Notes

Notes

Notes

Notes

Notes

Notes

Notes

Notes

Notes

Notes

Notes

Notes

Notes

Notes

Notes

Notes

Notes

Notes

Notes

Notes

Notes

Notes

Notes

Notes

Notes

Notes

Notes

Notes

Notes

Notes

Notes

Notes

Notes

Notes

Notes

Notes

Notes

Notes

Notes

Notes

Notes

Notes

Notes

Notes

Notes

Notes

Notes

Notes

Notes

Notes

Notes

Notes

Notes

Notes

Notes

Notes

Notes

Notes

Telephone Numbers

Telephone Numbers

Telephone Numbers

Telephone Numbers

Telephone Numbers

Telephone Numbers

We channel our artist creativity into creating wonderful gift ideas and writing aids for the thinker and the doer in all of us!

We've got something for everyone, from child to teen to adult, for the friend, the special occasion, stocking stuffers, office gifts, and gift basket goodies!

Take a look at our line of
- Planners
- Notebooks
- Journals
- Coloring Books
- Diaries
- Gratitude Journals
- Prayer Books
- and More

JournalInkPress.com

MyColorBooks.com

Thank you for supporting Independent Artists!

Copyright © 2017 by Journal Ink Press. All Rights Reserved.
Copyright © 2017 by MandaLove Press. All Rights Reserved.
Unauthorized duplication is strictly prohibited.

www.ingramcontent.com/pod-product-compliance
Lightning Source LLC
Chambersburg PA
CBHW070250230526
45470CB00002B/552